Level 2

# The Nature Kid's Guide to
# PRAYING MANTISES

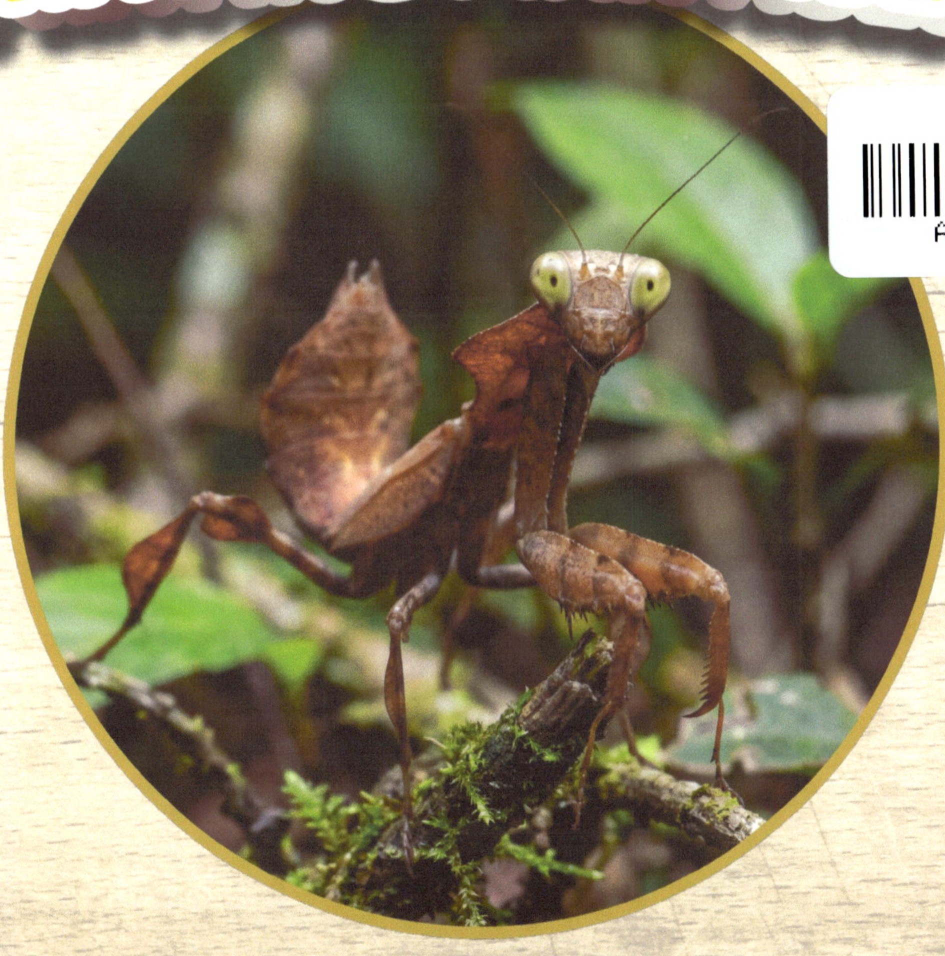

## DAVID ANDERSON

LP Media Inc. Publishing
Text copyright © 2026 by LP Media Inc.
All rights reserved.

No part of this book may be reproduced or transmitted in any form or by any means, electronic or mechanical, including photocopying, recording, or by an information storage and retrieval system — except by a reviewer who may quote brief passages in a review to be printed in a magazine or newspaper — without permission in writing from the publisher.

For information address LP Media Inc. Publishing,
30012 Variolite St NW, Princeton MN 55371
www.lpmedia.org

Publication Data

Praying Mantises
The Nature Kid's Guide to Praying Mantises — First edition.

Summary: "Learn all about Praying Mantises, the Nature Kid Way"
— Provided by publisher.

ISBN: 979-8-89818-226-7

[1. Praying Mantises – Non-Fiction] I. Title.

Title: The Nature Kid's Guide to Praying Mantises

# CONTENTS

# GREEN GARDENS

## Snap! A praying mantis patiently waits for a bug to fly near.

Praying mantises live in gardens, fields, and forests. They love warm places with lots of plants. Green leaves and tall grass give them perfect spots to hide.

The Chinese mantis is one common kind you might find in your yard. It sits perfectly still on a stem or leaf. Its green body matches the plants around it so well that most bugs never see it coming.

Mantises need plants around them. Flowers bring in bugs to eat. A leafy garden is the perfect mantis home.

WORLD WIDE
FUN FACT!
There are over 2,400 different kinds of mantises in the world!

## Buzz! A mantis hunts near a bright flower in warm Asia.

Praying mantises are found on six of the seven continents. From tropical forests to sunny meadows, they show up almost everywhere. The only place too cold for them is Antarctica!

The giant Asian mantis lives in the warm forests and fields of Asia. It is big enough to catch and eat lizards, frogs, and even small birds!

Some mantises were brought to new places by people. Farmers wanted them to eat pest bugs. It worked! Now these skilled hunters live in countries all around the globe.

# TINY TITANS



The giant shield mantis can grow over 6 inches long—bigger than a dollar bill!

8

**Zip! A tiny orchid mantis dashes along a twig in the warm sun.**

Praying mantises come in many sizes. Some are as small as a paper clip. Others are as long as a new pencil!

The orchid mantis is one of the tiniest kinds. It is only about 2 inches long. Its legs look like soft pink flower petals, and it could easily sit in the palm of your hand.

The biggest mantises are powerful predators. The larger the mantis, the longer it tends to live — some survive for over a year.

Big or small, all mantises are fierce hunters.

# BODY BUILD

DID YOU KNOW?
A mantis can turn its head almost all the way around—up to 180 degrees!

**Swish! A spiny flower mantis swings its front legs up high.**

A mantis has three main body parts. It has a head, a middle part, and a long belly. Six legs help it climb and grab.

The front two legs are special. They have sharp spines like tiny saws. A mantis uses them to catch and hold prey tight. The spiny flower mantis has extra bumps on its body that help it look like a flower.

Big eyes and thin feelers sit on its triangle-shaped head. The feelers help it smell and touch. Every part of this bug's body is built for hunting.

# SUPER SIGHT

A mantis has five eyes! Two are big **compound eyes**, and three tiny simple eyes sit on top of its head.

## Whoosh! A ghost mantis spots a tiny moth flying at sunset.

A mantis has amazing eyesight. Its two big eyes can spot the tiniest movement. It can see a bug move from 60 feet away!

The ghost mantis has large eyes for seeing in dim light. Unlike most insects, a mantis can actually judge distance — it knows exactly how far away a bug is before it strikes. No wasted lunges, no missed meals.

A mantis sees in 3D, just like you do. Very few insects can do that. This sharp sight makes mantises some of the best bug hunters in the world.

# CLEVER CAMO



Forget blending in! The iridescent bark mantis shimmers like a living jewel in blue, violet, and gold!

## Shh! Can you see the mantis hiding on that brown leaf?

Many mantises use camouflage to stay safe. That means they blend in with the world around them. Some look just like leaves, sticks, or flowers.

The dead leaf mantis is one of the best hiders. Its flat, brown body looks exactly like a dried leaf. When it stays still, almost nothing can spot it.

The bark mantis looks so much like tree bark that scientists sometimes walk right past it!

This trick helps in two ways. It hides mantises from animals that want to eat them. It also lets them sneak up on prey without being seen.

# BUG BUFFET

Large mantises have been observed catching and eating small hummingbirds!

# Crunch! A big mantis chomps down on a crunchy cricket.

Praying mantises are pure **carnivores**. They hunt crickets, flies, moths, beetles, and anything else they can catch. A hungry mantis is never picky!

The giant Asian mantis can eat several insects in a single day. It snatches its meal with its powerful front legs and starts eating immediately, head first. A bug rarely gets a second chance to escape.

Mantises never eat plants. They only eat things that move. One wrong step near a mantis and a bug becomes lunch!

# SNEAKY STRIKE

**FUN FACT!**

Some mantises hunt at porch lights at night, grabbing bugs that gather around the glow.

## Zap! The orchid mantis strikes faster than you can blink.

A mantis is a patient hunter. It stays in one spot and waits for hours. When a bug comes close, the mantis strikes in a flash—in just 50 milliseconds!

The orchid mantis has a sneaky trick. It looks like a pretty pink flower. Bugs fly right to it looking for nectar, and then snap! The mantis grabs its meal.

Mantises do not chase their food. They wait and let prey come to them. This still and silent style works very well.

WATCH OUT
20

# Swoop! A hungry bird dives down toward the little mantis.

Even a tough mantis can become a meal. Birds, bats, frogs, and spiders all eat mantises. Big insects can attack them too.

The ghost mantis is small and easy to miss. Its dark color helps it hide from hungry eyes. But if a bird spots it, the mantis must act fast.

Bats are especially dangerous at night. They use sound to find bugs in the dark. That is why mantises must always stay alert for danger.

Frogs can snatch a mantis right off a leaf with their long, sticky tongues!

# STAY STILL

Some mantises make a loud hissing sound by rubbing their wings together to scare enemies away!

## Freeze! The mantis holds perfectly still on its thin twig.

When danger is near, a mantis has tricks. The first trick is to freeze in place. A frozen mantis looks like part of the plant.

The dead leaf mantis drops to the ground and plays dead. It lies flat and looks just like a leaf on the forest floor. Most animals walk right past without noticing.

If freezing does not work, some mantises flash bright colors under their wings. This sudden surprise can scare a predator for a moment. That gives the mantis time to escape.

# CREEP CRAWL

Mantises can walk on ceilings and hang upside down from leaves—their feet grip like tiny hooks!

**Tap, tap! A mantis creeps along a thin green stem.**

Mantises are slow and careful walkers. They move on their four back legs. Their front legs stay raised and ready to grab.

The spiny flower mantis sways as it walks. This rocking motion makes it look like a petal blowing in the breeze. It helps the mantis sneak closer to prey without being noticed.

Some mantises can fly short distances. Males fly more than females because they are lighter. But most of the time, mantises prefer to walk or climb.

# DAY LIFE

DID YOU KNOW?
A mantis drinks water by sipping tiny drops of morning dew from leaves!

**Chirp! Morning birds sing as a mantis wakes on a warm leaf.**

A mantis has a simple daily routine — and it is surprisingly effective. Most of the day is spent perfectly still on a leaf or branch, watching, waiting, and letting breakfast come to it. For a mantis, patience is a superpower.

Between hunts, the Chinese mantis takes time to groom. It rubs its front legs across its eyes and face the same way a cat washes its whiskers. A clean mantis is a sharp-eyed mantis.

As darkness falls, the hunt pauses. The mantis presses close to a branch and goes quiet. At sunrise, the whole routine starts over.

# LONE LURKERS

## Hush! One lone mantis waits all by itself in the weeds.

Praying mantises live alone. They do not travel in groups or packs. Each mantis finds its own spot to sit and hunt.

A dead leaf mantis hides by itself on the forest floor. It does not need help from others. Living alone means there is no one to share food with—or steal it.

If two mantises meet, they might fight. The bigger one may even eat the smaller one! That is why mantises keep their distance from each other.

# RISKY ROMANCE

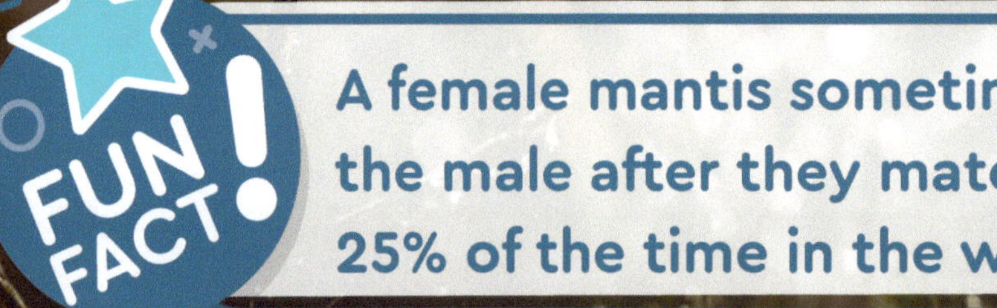


A female mantis sometimes eats the male after they mate—about 25% of the time in the wild!

## Flutter! A male mantis flies off to find his mate.

Mating is risky for a male mantis. The female is often bigger and stronger. The male must sneak up very slowly and carefully.

The Chinese mantis male is much smaller than the female. He creeps close when she is busy eating. If he is not careful, she may grab him instead!

After mating, the male quickly flies away. He must leave fast to stay safe. The female goes back to hunting, ready for her next meal.

# SOLO START

DID YOU KNOW?
A mantis egg case is so tough that rain, snow, and even freezing cold cannot break it!

## Poof! The mother mantis creates her egg case, then is gone forever.

A mother mantis does not raise her babies. She makes a foam egg case called an **ootheca**, then walks away. The hard foam keeps the eggs safe all winter long.

The giant Asian mantis makes one of the biggest egg cases. It can hold up to 400 eggs! She picks a safe branch and coats her eggs in foam. After that, she leaves and never comes back.

No parent waits for the babies to hatch. Each tiny **nymph** is on its own from the very start. Only the strongest will survive.

# MINI MANTIS

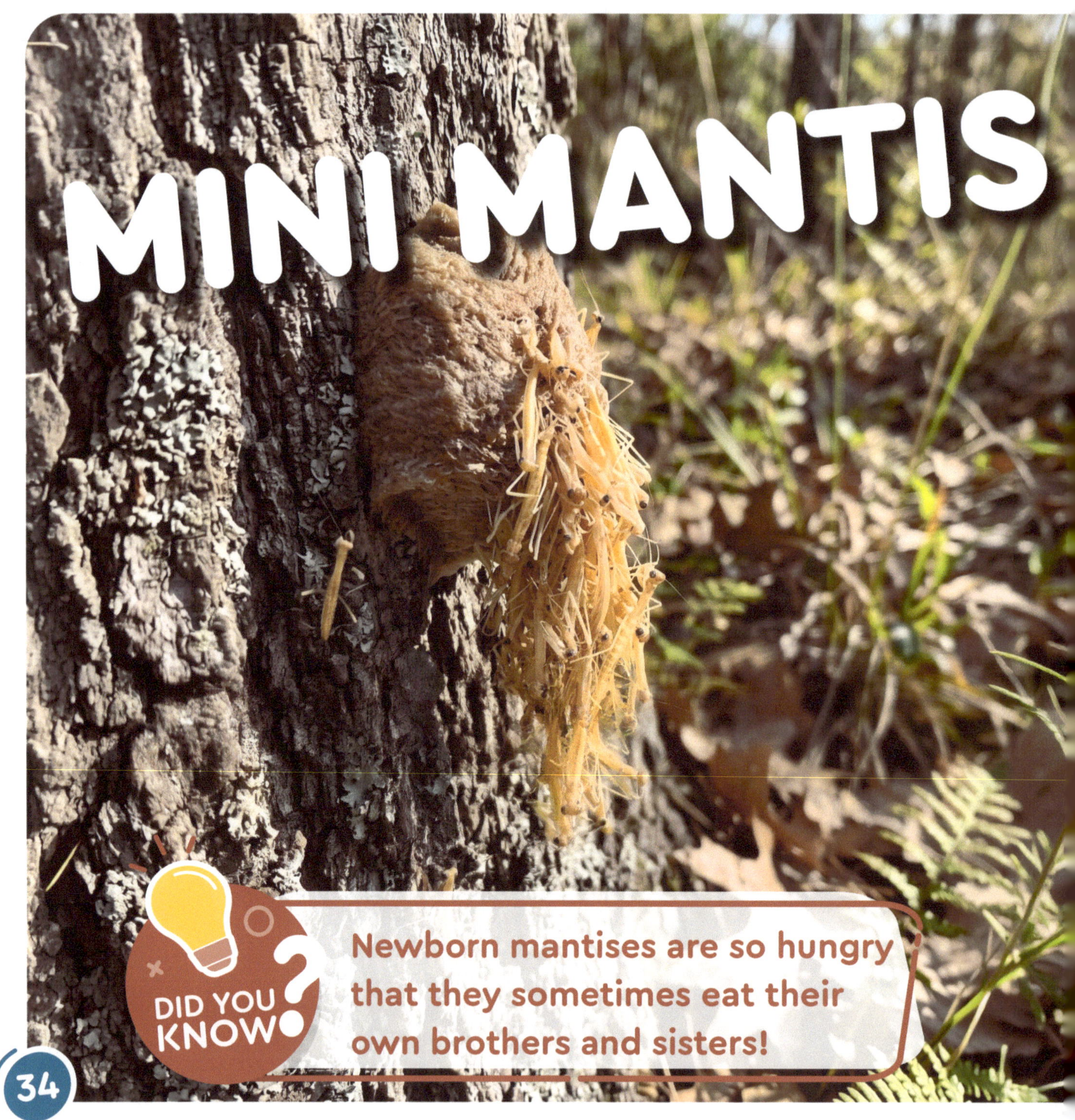

DID YOU KNOW?
Newborn mantises are so hungry that they sometimes eat their own brothers and sisters!

## Crack! Tiny baby mantises crawl out of their egg case.

In spring, a single egg case can release hundreds of tiny baby mantises all at once. These babies are called nymphs. It is one of the most dramatic hatching events in the insect world!

The nymphs must find food fast. They hunt tiny bugs like gnats and fruit flies almost immediately after hatching. As they grow, they shed their skin over and over in a process called **molting**. Each molt reveals a bigger, stronger body underneath.

After three to six months of eating, molting, and hunting, the nymph is finally a full-grown adult — ready to start the whole cycle again.

# ANCIENT ALIENS

## Whir! A mantis flaps its wings, just like bugs long ago.

Praying mantises are survival experts. Every part of their body seems purpose-built to hunt, hide, and stay alive.

The ghost mantis is one of the most remarkable examples. Its body is covered in strange leaf-like shapes that break up its outline and baffle predators. To a passing animal, it looks just like a pile of dead leaves.

These ancient hunters have outlasted countless other creatures on Earth. Their tricks — speed, stillness, camouflage, and patience — have kept them going longer than almost any other insect alive today.

SPOT THEM
FUN FACT!
The praying mantis is the official state insect of Connecticut!

## Psst! Look close at that branch. Can you spot the mantis?

You can look for mantises in your own yard! Check flowers, bushes, and tall weeds. Summer and fall are the best times to spot them.

Look for something that does not quite match. A spiny flower mantis may look like a bloom, but watch for tiny legs. If a flower seems to move, look again!

Be slow and quiet when you get close. Mantises scare easily and may fly off. If you are patient, you might see one resting perfectly still—waiting for its next meal.

# GLOSSARY

### ootheca

The foam egg case a female mantis makes to keep her eggs safe

### nymph

A baby insect that has not grown up yet.

### molting

When an insect sheds its old skin to grow a bigger, new one

### compound eyes

Eyes made up of hundreds of tiny lenses packed together

### carnivore

An animal that eats only meat and never plants

www.ingramcontent.com/pod-product-compliance
Lightning Source LLC
Chambersburg PA
CBHW041618110726
48005CB00002B/435